MW01088996

A Calendar of Care

A Calendar *of* Care

Reflections of a Country Pastor

James Schmitmeyer

Liturgy Training Publications
National Catholic Rural Life Conference

Cover photographs: Church by Ron Yee-Mon; potting by Patrick Murphy-Racey; sandbagging by Bruce Crummy. Photo on page 9 by Shirley Henderson; on page 23 © Bill Whitman; on page 39 by Tim Wenzl; on page 53 by James Bowey.

Parts of the introduction were published in "The Beauty of Holiness," in Assembly, March 1993, pp. 594 – 5. Used with permission.

The hymn, "God, Whose Farm Is All Creation," on page 1, © John Arlott. Reprinted with permission. It can be found in Worship, third edition, GIA Publications, Inc., Chicago.

"Seasons and Processions" was first published as "Such Are Our Processions" in Liturgy 90, October 1995, p. 8.

The following chapters were first published in and are copyrighted by the New Oxford Review: "Lenten Wood, Easter Fire" (March 1998); "In the Country" (September 1997); "A Season of Grace, A Season of Thieves" (December 1998). Reprinted with permission of the New Oxford Review, 1069 Kains Avenue, Berkeley CA 94706.

"Coyote Wind" was first published under the title "Rural Communities Support Their Habit" in America, October 21, 1995, pp. 6 – 7. Reprinted with permission.

"Harvest Prophets" was first published in The Catholic Telegraph, November 28, 1997.

Articles from the Greenville Daily Advocate reprinted by permission. All rights reserved. Names and other identifying characteristics of persons in "Scenes from a Search" have been changed to protect privacy.

A CALENDAR OF CARE: REFLECTIONS OF A COUNTRY PASTOR © 1999 Archdiocese of Chicago: Liturgy Training Publications, 1800 North Hermitage Avenue, Chicago IL 60622-1101; 1-800-933-1800; orders @ltp.org; www.ltp.org; fax 1-800-933-7094. All rights reserved.

This book was edited by Victoria M. Tufano. Audrey Novak Riley was the production editor. It was designed by Lucy Smith and typeset in Gill Sans and Bernard Modern by Karen Mitchell. It was printed in Canada by Webcom Limited.

Library of Congress Card Number: 99-067135

ISBN 1-56854-339-5

CALCAR

03 02 01 00   5 4 3 2

To Jake Buschur

Contents

Foreword

Love of the land and its people is what makes a space become a place. The people spoken of by Father James Schmitmeyer are people who feel a sense of belonging to the land and to each other. They live amidst rhythms of seasons, of spring, summer, fall and winter, as well as seasons of hope and hardship. These people of the land have much to teach all of us in our busyness and sometimes frenetic desperation. They can teach us to suffer and to celebrate. Learning these human rhythms brings us a depth and a balance. When appreciated in the broader context of care for animals and care for the earth itself, these rhythms can teach us much about life's deeper channels and cycles.

A Jesuit philosopher, Father Bernard Lonergan, once wrote that the geography, economy and religious culture of a locale provide us a glimpse of its uniqueness as a whole way of life. Each locale with its unique combination of people, land, animals and plants is an interdependent web of life. If we could learn to laugh and cry like the people of the land depicted in these pages, we could learn a deeper spiritual richness to life. That's what Father Schmitmeyer is doing in these pages, providing a grounding in spirituality and community as lived in a particular web of life. The experience there has much to teach everyone everywhere. A rural community, in its belonging together, its appreciation of a particular landscape, can teach us all how our own landscapes might — perhaps ought to — be.

Enjoy the people and places whose stories are shared within these pages. They'll lead you out of yourself into another set of lives, and give wisdom and insight so that you can return enriched to your own home.

Brother David Andrews, CSC
Executive Director
The National Catholic Rural Life Conference
Des Moines, Iowa

Acknowledgments

This book is a small token of the affection
I hold for the people of Osgood and North Star. They
are the primary inspiration for this book.

I am grateful for the commitment to rural
communities on the part of my archbishop, the Most
Reverend Daniel Pilarczyk, and for the support and
encouragement of many colleagues, particularly Father
Timothy Bunch, Brian Henties, Sister Christine Pratt,
Brother David Andrews and the staff of the National
Catholic Rural Life Conference.

I also wish to extend a special thanks to Lori
Poeppelman for her assistance in preparing the
manuscript.

Introduction

A Calendar of Care

God, whose farm is all creation,
Take the gratitude we give;
Take the finest of our harvest
Crops we grow that all may live.

Take our plowing, seeding, reaping,
Hopes and fears of sun and rain,
All our thinking, planning, waiting,
Ripened in this fruit and grain.

All our labor, all our watching,
All our calendar of care,
In these crops of your creation,
Take, O God, they are our prayer.

It was early evening. A mercury lamp shone down the edge of the silo. A young farmer named Steve climbed out of the cab of his tractor and stood in the bluish light. Wedges of shadow cut across his strong body and tired face.

I got out of my truck and walked across the gravel to where he stood.

My sheep were out of hay, and I had come to ask for some. Steve had had a good third cutting and would be willing to spare some bales. His wife called from the barn and soon joined us. The dangerous season of night work was coming to an end. It was Saturday and they were quitting early, but there was no hurry to get to the house. Their voices sounded smooth in the cool air; a phrase spoken here and there in the common ritual of neighbors. No information required, just the slow speech of the rural Midwest, full of soft, easy silences.

Beth went on into the house, and Steve and I set off for the barn.

As we walked he mentioned the return of his nephew's leukemia.

"Greg's boy?" I asked.

"Yeah," he said, and his voice was suddenly heavy. "Bone marrow transplant," he went on. "That's the only hope now."

"That's a serious procedure," I replied, as we continued walking. "He's a brave kid," I added.

"Trying to be."

"Sixteen?"

"Seventeen, now."

We reached the barn but didn't go in.

Steve leaned on a gate and looked across the fields toward the lights of the village. "He could die," he said evenly. "There's only one chance. If it fails, he'll die."

We stood there awhile in the silence. The bells of the church began ringing in the distance.

That night the air was clear.

And we could hear more than the distant bells.

It is a rare privilege to share such moments in the lives of God's people, though I am sure that most ministers can cite many similar instances. I suspect that it is the grace encountered in such moments — when the presence of Mystery becomes nearly palpable — that compels those of us in pastoral work to continue our labor of love.

This book is an attempt to capture something of the grace I have been privileged to witness as a pastor of two rural parishes in west central Ohio. This grace is not, of course, the private domain of those who happen to be involved in pastoral ministry. I am acutely aware that my words only dimly mirror the profound experience of God's presence in the lives of my parishioners.

In this respect, the chapters of this book revisit the universal questions that confront every believer: the quest for meaning, the need for hope in the face of uncertainty, the experience of joy in the simple things of life. But since these reflections are placed within a particular setting, they offer a unique perspective on those universal themes. These chapters offer an intimate portrayal of a rural parish confronting some of the most disquieting issues in our society today: the diminishing role of community, the effects of a global economy, the horror of violence.

How might these rural reflections benefit Christians living in cities and suburbs as well as small towns? As a country pastor, I have come to see that rural people have a certain gift to share with the rest of the church. Ours is a life where there are persistent reminders that there is an underlying rhythm to life, one rooted in nature and determined by the changes of the seasons. Ours is a spirituality that responds to the alternating moods of the weather, the varying needs of the community, and the enduring rituals of planting and harvest.

Unfortunately, this rhythmic dimension of life, even in a rural setting, is increasingly divorced from nature's pace. Schedules are packed and the demands of work are overbearing. Yet, even in the midst of a hectic life, people everywhere continue to rely on underlying rhythms to bring some sense of order to life's activities: the stages of childhood development, the succession of athletic seasons, the fiscal reports at work, the birthdays and anniversaries at home.

Whether our environment is rural, urban or suburban, most of us recognize the value of the calendars that shape our progress through life. The frantic respone to the loss of an appointment book clearly shows the need for the pacing and predictability that calendars, schedules and deadlines provide.

For those who believe in God, there are additional ways to instill a sense of order. Prayer, fasting and feasting bring a sense of meaning to events that both bless and buffet us. The recurrence of days that are designated as holy, the overlay of seasons that are penitential or joyful, the hours of the day that are marked for praise or thanksgiving provide additional cushioning, a chance to take a breath, a time to ponder and to give thanks to the One in whom we live and move and have our being.

But for Christians who live in a rural area, this liturgical calendar is directly connected to another, more fundamental system of ordering time: the schedule of nature itself, which, in the Northern Hemisphere, precedes and undergirds the liturgical celebrations of the church. It is lovingly described in the words of John Arlott's hymn, "God Whose Farm Is All Creation," as "our calendar of care," an ancient and primordial way of observing the phases of the moon and the movement of feasts. It is the first of all calendars and the one that retains the strongest emphasis on the relationship between the divine ordering of nature and the human ordering of time.

It is, in a way, an interior calendar rooted in the seasons of the year but adjusted to the experiences of one's faith. Although its nearest relative is the liturgical calendar, it exists prior to and separate from it. It is the calendar of the natural seasons and the undulating patterns they impose on a community through the demands of climate, the timing of cultivation and the distribution of the harvest. It plays a role in how a community remains viable and, when honored, it produces colonies of compassion, where the ancient connections between soil and harvest, water and life, labor and love remain clearly discernable in the pacing and rhythm of human life.

This is the gift that my two parishes have given to me and the one I wish to pass on to you. You may not begin and end your day by feeding a flock of sheep in a barn as I do, nor cut wood to heat your house, nor toll a bell when someone in your community dies. But I am sure you will find in the pages of this book an opportunity for the calendar of nature to work its influence on the patterns and rhythms of your own life.

Cultivating this awareness will allow you to hear not only the bells of a church in the distance, but also the silent voice of God within and between your time at work, your time at home and your time at prayer.

Spring

Seasons and Processions

We know many kinds of processions. Some move with the solemnity of a deep river. Others rush with the energy of rapids or skim by like stones skipped on the surface of a pond.

In the spring, children sing, green branches floating above their hosannas like leaves carried on a meandering creek. We float forward to pour canned goods into baskets for the hungry, we walk barefoot to be washed, we walk bearing bread. We stream to the wood of the cross. All of us shuffle in the dark behind the pillar of fire, toward the word and the water. Wet neophytes leave footprints on the floor and chrism's scent in the air.

And then it is May. Other processions sweep into their currents whatever is at hand: lilacs or dandelions, glass beads or plastic, an image borne aloft, children in white, grandmothers in shawls, even knights (of Columbus) brandishing swords.

There are marches of memorial, parades of patriotism, and lines of cars headed to the shore. So moves summer, until workers walk instead of work, laborers and clerks streaming out of factories and offices, down city streets and into autumn.

We know other processions, too. There are those with the dead: The grieving bear the body, straining to hear the greetings of martyrs, leaning to hear the welcome of angels, their sore arms locked, their shoulders propped against each other for the march.

One November, on All Souls, the parish gathered in the cemetery to pray for the dead. Incense rose before the cross, and the clouds of rain hung low and gray in the west. In the crowd stood a young dairy farmer who, a few weeks ago, had buried his friend in this ground. His friend had moved away — to the city — but his body was returned to the land on which he had been raised. For many nights before and after the funeral, the young farmer relieved his dead friend's family of hours of labor with the herd, working in their barn from midnight until three, only to begin tending his own cows at four.

This, too, was procession: him trudging to the barn at midnight, friends in mourning awkwardly approaching the door of the house, offering solace and help with the chores. Now these very same people, who then had come in ones and twos, now huddled in the cemetery against a bitter November wind with faces set cold and hard like gravestones, eyes looking for some light to break through the clouds. We gazed at brown fields, remembering the gold wheat that had swayed there, remembering the hands that had worked there, the feet that had walked there, the lips, the skin, the smell of the hair, the sound of a voice borne on the wind and the call of a name at supper time.

House to barn to field to home — such are our processions. The women go down to church to sew garments for the poor during Lent. The men arrive with hammers and lumber amid the charred ruins of a neighbor's barn. Such are our processions: the trickling streams and moving rivers that carry us, push us shoulder to shoulder like the gang of children that we are, playing and splashing in the baptism of Spirit, crying and laughing. Such are our processions: from strength to strength, year to year turning the arid valley into a place of springs, making the dry sojourn a river of grace.

Lenten Wood, Easter Fire

I remember one day, as a child, running toward
a tree I wanted to climb, then stopping suddenly to stare
in disbelief at the giant thorns sprouting all over its trunk.
This was my first sight of a locust tree. It was growing
along a fencerow that my father was clearing at the back
of our farm.

The thorns on a locust tree can be ten inches in length,
with secondary thorns sprouting out of the larger spikes.
They grow in ghastly clusters all about the trunk of the tree
and singly along the branches and twigs.

As a woodsman I have had to contend with the
physical aspects of locust trees through the years, but my
first encounter was entirely theological. Why God would
ever create such a sinister tree was beyond my reckoning.

Noticing my stunned reaction to the sight of that
tree, my father laid aside his axe and pulled down a branch

for my inspection. "These are dangerous thorns," he said protectively. Then added, "They're the kind that were used on Jesus."

They did, indeed, look like the pictures I had seen in our Bible. I nodded my agreement. My father then took his axe to the tree. As he swung at the trunk, I looked for a place to run when that wicked tree would give its final shudder and fall to the earth. I was happy when its thorns fell to the ground in a slow, creaking scream of defeat.

Since that time I have come to realize that the locust has its uses: Its wood is quite resistant to moisture and makes durable fence posts. But I have also learned that the people of Appalachia call it the Jesus Tree. I find this ability to evoke the Passion to be its most valuable quality.

This is especially apparent to me each Holy Week when I make a trek to a wooded gully near my village to gather cedar wood for the Easter fire.

This gully has become for me a lenten chapel. Each year it provides a day of recollection as the Triduum draws near. Its outer edges are steep and crowded with locusts. But the thorn trees soon give way to thick underbrush which, like Lent itself, is difficult to negotiate. Finally, in the center of the grove are the cedars. Their lower branches are dead, brittle and gray. They extend from the trunks like hundreds of crosses. Along this journey from thorns to crosses, long strands of berry bushes arc red and smooth like streams of blood. Despite my best efforts, stickers tear at my jeans and the skin on the back of my hands.

This year I have come with a friend named Jake, whose family owns the farm in which the gully is located. He walks ahead of me with a chainsaw in hand and a maul over his shoulder. I carry a jug of oil and a container of fuel.

As we enter the grove he is talking about an article he read on near-death experiences. We converse in serious tones about faith and science, endorphins and Resurrection. I am somewhat distracted, however, as I search for some wood that will ignite easily come Saturday night.

As we move deeper into the prickly thickets, the topic of death persists. I find myself reluctantly thinking of my mother and her recent passing.

She died in November, a few days before the Feast of Christ the King. As always in that closing season of the year, the readings spoke of the last things and of Christ the Judge coming at the end of time.

For my mother, however, that final week was all mercy and grace. She experienced very little pain. There was no struggle or fear. Despite her peaceful death, however, the memories of that week continue to pierce me like thorns — the heaving of her chest, the feather-like weight of her hand, her final breath, the sound of our prayers for angels to greet her and martyrs to meet her — all of it as vivid and sharp as this spring day amid thorns and thickets and theological tangles.

Eventually, Jake and I enter a clearing where his father had felled a cedar last summer. Jake says that it was dead when his father cut it down, therefore seasoned enough to burn well on the night of the Vigil. I start the chain saw and begin trimming the branches. As I cut into its trunk, the air fills with the fragrance of the cedar wood. I kick away sections of the tree with my boot. Its inner core is a deep purple, like lenten vestments, or in some places a reddish pink, as if stained with blood.

As my saw tears hungrily into the wood, Jake's ungloved hands — farmer hands — pull the branches into a pile. He takes the maul and begins to split the scattered pieces of trunk.

He continues to chop as I turn off the saw and stand in the sudden quiet. I listen to the soothing knock of the maul against the wood, the cracking sound of soft cedar splitting. The fragrance again rises like incense, its sacrifice like the lifting up of hands, like the lifting up of the cross beam on Calvary.

I study my friend and admire his strength and his life. His friendship strengthens my faith. He is Simon of Cyrene coming in from the fields. He is a carpenter and sower, a trapper and tiller, a husband and provider. Always at hand, always at work.

I am his friend and his pastor and the pastor of many who are like him, people of the country, women and children and men, quiet and humble and devoted to Christ — the Christ who, in this Holy Week, will shoulder his cross and bleed in our liturgy, the gash in his side as red as opened cedar, his skin as purple and torn as Lent.

I know I am on holy ground in this woods and in this community. I move among the people of my parish unworthily, washing their feet, anointing their hands and heads with oil, baptizing their young, burying their dead. I am their priest, their brother Abel, their tree-trimming Amos, their tent-making Paul.

Few priests are as privileged as I. I come from the same land as my parishioners. Our homesteads were cleared, our towns built, our churches constructed from the same forests. My initials are carved in the beech trees here, I swam in the creeks beneath the spreading sycamores, our farms were interlocked, our families inter-related. Our hunting, our drinking, our fumbling are all the same — so much am I one of them.

Yet, in this Holy Week, we are joined even closer, joined like the grain of the wood in the cross we touch and kiss on Good Friday. We will huddle together on the night of Holy Saturday. Faces will glow with the warmth of the fire. Glances will be cast toward the night sky by eyes that somehow know that the fire outside our dark-ened church burns brighter than all the stars of heaven. For on this night earth will exult and the holy church will resound with joy at the rising of Christ from the darkness of the tomb.

Each year we gather for these transforming rites. Each year Christ's own presence fills the holy night. Our souls are transfixed and our wounded Savior is transfigured. He is jubilant and muscular and fierce, with thorn-pierced scalp and wood-scraped skin, his eyes reflecting the flames of our fire.

I send up the cry, "Christ our Light!"

"Thanks be to God," they respond.

The crowd grows silent. The cedar crackles.

"Christ our Light!" I sing again.

"Thanks be to God!"

The chant rises to the trees and soon echoes in the church as we process inside. It drifts to the vaults of the ceiling and settles in the niches of the altars. In the night air inside the church it ruffles the cloak of the Risen One. He rises above us, silent and strong, breathing like the stallion in Job, his black eyes ablaze, a champion.

The chanting caresses his wounds. Soon the ancient scriptures are read, stories of water and tears, death and redemption. Soon our fingers, brown with blood, will reach for the water of the font, our eyes yearning to see eternal life glinting on its surface, our minds grasping its power — Christ's own power — to cleanse and renew, to bring forth from dead wood the ever-new, the ever-breathing life of God.

These are the mysteries we celebrate on a spring night when clouds float blue and gray across a full moon. The vigilant mysteries that press against our windows in the dark of night, the quiet peace beneath the mournful wind we hear in our trees.

The Lord is here, risen indeed, risen in our land, in our towns, in our sheds, in our history and in our love. In the smell of cedar and the fragrance of incense. In the waters of baptism and rivers and lakes, in the relics of the dead and the songs of the saints. This Woodsman and Farmer, this Neighbor and Bridegroom, this Stallion, this Champion, this Priest, this Friend.

Summer

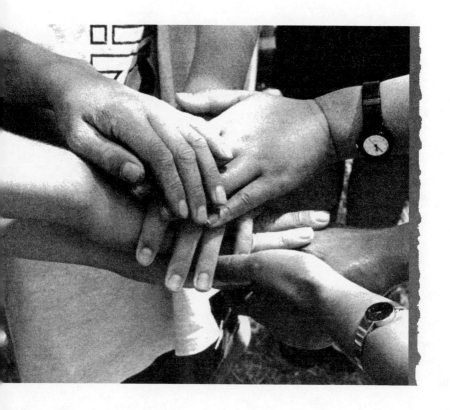

In the Country

"Where are your sheep, Father?" Jay asks as he throws another rock on the pile behind the barn.

"They got mad and left," I respond as I try with a hoe to pry loose a slab of cement. "They got tired of this rocky manure yard and decided to go to the city. I think they're headed for Chicago."

"Father, priests aren't supposed to lie."

Jay is ten years of age and old enough to provide some direction to misguided adults.

"I'm just telling you what they had on their minds. You don't see them around anywhere, do you?"

"So where are they?"

"They took a bus for Chicago. I bought them all a ticket and off they went. Didn't even say good-bye."

"Father! I told you priests aren't supposed to lie."

"It's the truth, Jay, they didn't have the courtesy to say good-bye. When was the last time you heard a sheep say good-bye?"

"Father!"

"Come help me lift this slab, Jay."

"Father, where are the sheep?"

"Well, if you want to know the truth, they're hanging out on the edge of Yorkshire, in Broerman's pasture. But for all they know, it could be the skyline of Chicago they're looking at."

"Oh, so they think tiny Yorkshire is really Chicago?"

"I won't tell them if you don't."

"And I guess the Greyhound bus was that red and gray truck of yours," he says, nodding toward the barnyard, glad to be in on the joke.

I lean on my hoe and study his face. He smiles as he tosses a rock from hand to hand. His head is tilted back and his eyes sparkle with all the light of summer.

"You ready to ride Levi when we're through?" I ask.

"You mean it?"

"You'll have to keep him in the round pen."

"Cool!"

An elderly couple used to live on this farm. They were holy people. Claude would rise early to begin his prayers, and Margaret would soon join him. In this part of Ohio, where full-time farmers generally till 800 to 1,000

acres, Margaret and Claude made their living off a scant seven. Claude drove a school bus on the side; Margaret occasionally worked in a canning factory in the summertime.

About a year ago, on a First Friday, I was closing the prayer book and preparing to leave Claude's bedside when he said to me, "I have next to nothing, Father."

"What do you mean?" I asked.

"I don't have much to show for my life," he said.

I tried to be reassuring. "All the easier to get into heaven, Claude," I said.

He continued to look anxious.

"You've lived your whole life with trust in God," I said. "Are you worried about Margaret? You can trust God to look after Margaret."

"She's moving to Dayton with our daughter," he said.

"She's told me." I took his hand in mine. "She's told me she's well set."

"I have nothing," he said again.

"Soon you'll have everything."

"I did my best," he said and closed his eyes. "No big silos on this place," he added.

"'Things that rust corrodes and moths destroy,' eh, Claude?"

He smiled and gave a small laugh. "Take what you need and leave the rest. That's what I've always said."

"It's what you always lived."

God called Claude to eternal life the following week. More than 600 people attended his wake.

Claude and Margaret's farm was purchased by a parishioner. Soon after the funeral I decided to rent the farm buildings and the seven-acre field. The place now carries the name of Saint Maria, the wife of Saint Isidore, the patron of farmers. She is revered for her generosity and for always sharing food from her table with the poor, even though she and Isidore were very poor themselves.

In the front yard of the farm there's a picture of Saint Maria holding a basket of food. The sign announces that eggs, fresh produce and compost are for sale. All the proceeds are given to the poor.

A retired couple, Slim and Mary Jean, oversee the feeding and care of the 100 hens who cluck away in an old-fashioned coop. I gather the eggs every day at noon. Other parishioners donate fruit and vegetables for the produce stand.

My own garden is late this year and full of weeds. Fortunately, it is tucked out of view behind the chicken coop. I've always been better with livestock than with plants, and I am presently having good success raising lambs for my own table.

In good weather I often ride one of my horses to the parish office. In recent years horseback riding has become very popular in our area. I usually spend Sunday afternoons riding along Mile Creek or the Wabash River with friends.

Some kids from the youth ministry helped me build a round pen earlier this spring, and I've begun to train and sell colts to pay the rent on what was once Claude and Margaret's farm.

❧

"Frankly, you farmers are just afraid of competition. And I suspect that most of you are just upset because you're missing out on a good deal!"

The local politician was proclaiming his faith in corporate-controlled agribusiness, explaining that the market determines what is best for everyone and that inefficient farmers have to be weeded out.

The pork producers attending the public forum were angry and began shouting back.

"Soon there won't be any more of us to weed out," they said. "The corporations will shut us out of the market! They did it in North Carolina — they'll do it here."

Heads nodded in agreement.

"They own the hogs, they own the trucking, they own the processing plants. They'll end up owning us!"

"You have to understand," said the politician from his high podium, "this is a consumer-driven economy, and consumers demand lean meat and low prices."

"We're not just consumers," shouted someone from the back of the room. "We're citizens. Citizens demand fairness and the right to live in communities where the living is good!"

"I spent three hours with the owners of the corporation," declared the politician, "and they're good people, they're decent people."

"You're for the bloodsuckers, aren't you?" another person yelled. "People who suck the lifeblood out of our towns and out of our farms and pay a penny a gallon! And once the blood's gone, they pack up and leave!"

Color was rising to people's faces; the meeting was called to a hasty end. As usual, the politician had the last word. "It's a global economy, folks. Get used to it. It's a consumer-driven world."

At Saint Maria's Farm parishioners (as opposed to consumers) often stop to chat, a rather inefficient activity from an economic point of view.

Not long ago a fellow named Paul, a dairy farmer in his early 30s, pulled in to tell me of his recent engagement. I looked at Paul and told him I thought it was about time he got married. We went on to talk about the wet spring and the dry summer.

We then climbed to the loft, and I showed him the hay I had baled the week before. He looked at me and told me it was about time I did something with that ugly field.

"We're even," I told him.

Paul began to talk about his fiancée wanting to become Catholic and the importance of faith in his future marriage. I mentioned praying together. He said, "We've already started doing that." I knew he wasn't kidding.

Down from the loft, he stood with his hands on his hips, looking at the barn, and said, "This place has *fun* written all over it."

He was exactly right, except he meant to use the word *grace*.

In the country, children can ride on ponies. And sheep can ride on buses as easily as politicians can swagger. In the country people hunt and trap and fish. The soil is rich and food is not wasted.

In the country a pastor can work in the fields with no shirt on his back and feel the Spirit warming his shoulders.

In the country they drink lots of beer at reunions, and they square dance at weddings. In the summer they have campfires with the neighbors and fireworks for the kids. In the country the bells of the Angelus are borne on the wind, and processions with Mary flow through the towns like meandering creeks.

In the country people have no idea of what holy icons they are, with the glow of fire on their faces, the golden sun on their horizons.

In the country they have no idea how deeply the passion of Christ shines in their eyes.

Coyote Wind

In 1988 I left a faculty position at a graduate school of theology and became a rural pastor. This brought me back to my home region, a part of Ohio known for its small communities and neatly kept family farms.

Many of my parishioners, like a majority of farmers, now rely on off-farm income, a way of "supporting their habit," as they put it. Still, the local economy remains primarily agricultural, lending a rare cohesion and solidarity to our communities.

While my urban colleagues struggle with the effects of individualism in parish life, I find myself enjoying the benefits of a true community — heating my house with wood that I cut and split with friends, growing my own meat in a parishioner's pasture, joining with neighbors to replace a barn that has burned down, milking cows for a young husband and father injured in a farm accident, chatting with the women in the church hall sewing blankets for the poor during Lent.

Instead of attending symposiums on globalism, I now go square dancing at weddings, get sunburned in the fields and bless rosaries and animals and seeds.

Such is the life in the communities where I live, where the roads bear the names of our grandparents and great-grandparents; where a physical trait ties you to a host of relatives; where, at the time of a death, people gather laden with food and sorrow and the memories that draw forth from us a profound sense of dignity in who we are and who we are for one another.

Yet, as in countless rural towns across the country, there is something disquieting in the air. Like the yelp of coyotes at nightfall, we hear the eerie and unsettling news that family-based farming is a thing of the past. Many agricultural leaders as well as elected officials seem to concur that corporations are now poised to take control of the last independent element of the food chain: the farmer.

We all know the jingle. It's been fed to us for two generations: "This is America, Mr. Greenjeans, get big or get out."

Some farmers respond with intense expanding of live-stock, facilities and land, not so much for money, but to try to ensure a place for their children in farming. Others respond by cutting the costs of inputs, investing study and increased labor into sustainable or organic practices.

Still others work in town, and farm at night and on the weekend.

But for all types of family farmers, the hedging of bets against the Goliaths of the agribusiness and food production industries would make even the stones in David's hands glisten with sweat.

So why not befriend the gentle giants of American enterprise we know so well?

Many farmers have done this. Virtually all the nation's poultry growers are now under contract to a handful of processors. Under these agreements, the corporations absorb the fluctuations of the market. In return, farmers are required to pay for buildings, equipment, land, labor costs and, when necessary, environmental clean-up.

This business-oriented solution, however, is reminiscent of the coal mining companies of the 1920s. In most contractual arrangements, the food or agribusiness firm not only "owns the company store," but a host of other things as well. For starters, it will own all the animals, except the dead ones. It will also have partial or complete ownership of an assortment of various other links in the food chain: the grain, the feed additives, the elevator, the medicine, the trucking and all the processing.

Most importantly, the companies control the management decisions, turning once-independent farmers into employees working on their own land, sometimes earning little more than the minimum wage. This practice of vertical integration, which entered the farm scene by reaching for the egg money, is now eyeing the mortgage itself as it quickly expands into the pork, beef, dairy and vegetable sectors as well.

Many will see this trend simply as free enterprise and the result of technological development. Unfortunately, they will not understand the delicate interdependence of local, rural economies where the family farmer returns nearly 90 percent of a year's income back to the local economy in taxes and farm-related purchases. Corporate-based agriculture, on average, returns less than half, and most of this is in wages.

To put it simply, when prevailing competitive arrangements prevent farmers' receiving a fair return on their investment and labor, rural towns languish and the number of working poor people in the United States, already disproportionately high in rural areas, continues to grow.

What I fear most, however, is a lack of vision on the part of our elected officials who will continue to evaluate what remains of the family farm by tired theories of "bigger is better," theories that ignore the communal dimension of rural life. This is the sort of thinking that has brought us polluted ground water in North Carolina, thinning topsoil in Iowa, countless ghost towns in the countryside and contaminated chicken at local stores.

Of course, there will be nothing as dramatic as the battles that pushed aside the Native Americans, only the coyote-like yelping of auctioneers followed by the silent packing up of belongings — and perhaps a suicide here and there — as each week 600 farm families are forced to give up a way of life that, in a just society, would be as profitable as it is ennobling.

There was a time when people in towns like mine were secure and prosperous. Despite the lack of a level playing field, however, many remain out of love for the land and their communities. I admire them deeply and emulate them as best I can. Tonight, for instance, I'll close my day as most of them do: I'll feed my livestock. I'll pray for the people I love. And I'll hope the sound of coyotes starts disturbing your sleep as much as it does mine.

Autumn

Harvest Prophets

The barns are broken down, the granaries lie in ruin." (Joel 1:17)

Rural nostalgia is in vogue. Bookstores have piles of gift books and calendars featuring quaint villages, country churches and old, weathered barns, all of them nestled in the colorful leaves in September and blankets of snow in December.

There are bank barns, prairie barns, octagonal barns, Amish barns. Summer light spilling through gaps in the siding as glorious as the light around Gabriel's wings. The lofts are swept clean. The geometry of beams and rafters forms patterns of elegant beauty.

These are the barns of gift books and calendar art. But the abandoned barns that I know have sagging doors and broken backs. They do not shimmer with silent songs

41

of beauty. They seem instead to chant the rough oracles of ancient prophets.

"Woe to you who add field to field and house to house," says Isaiah, "for you will soon dwell alone in the land and many houses, many large and beautiful houses, will stand empty." (5:8)

Abandoned barns and falling-down houses are a common sight in rural America these days. In the last 15 years, 367,000 farmers have left the land. Currently, more than 600 farms a week go out of business.

Like the prophets of old, abandoned homesteads make us ask disturbing questions, such as, "Who once lived here?" and "Why did they leave?"

For the prophets, the answers eventually focused on reverence for God, gratitude for food and proper treatment for those who labored on the land. When these things were missing, the farmers suffered, the cities suffered and all society suffered.

But such clarity of thought is hard to grasp today. Our former focus on land, families and communities is increasingly dominated by elements more germane to industry, management and profit-taking. We neglect reverence and are content with nostalgia.

Who cares if technology pushes people off the land? Who cares if wealth is concentrated in the hands of a few, in the hands of people who don't like getting their hands dirty?

Like bygone prophets of yesteryear, the abandoned barns, we think, have no modern-day value. After all, their wooden floors are rotten, and groundhogs and rats burrow beneath them.

In the Bible, it is different. God's gifts of land and food are of great importance, and attitudes about these gifts soon affect all of society.

In Genesis, we read how the farmers of Egypt said to Joseph, "Shall we die before your eyes? We have nothing left. Take our bodies and our farms and make us slaves of Pharaoh." (47:19)

We all know the story of Joseph's beautiful coat, and we teach it to our children. But do we remember his agricultural policies?

We have much to learn. Old barns and Bibles have much to say.

When you explore an abandoned barn, you are likely to find glass bottles or remnants of bottles on windowsills or behind worm-eaten posts. Some bottles held medicine, others whiskey — whiskey used for lambs born in a cold season or by a farmer dying in a bad one.

"Here crying aloud," says the apostle James, "are the wages withheld from the farmhand. . . ." (5:4)

Beneath the decay, however, a good eye can detect the pride that once swelled within these structures: the hand-hewn beams and hand-carved stanchions; a lingering coat of whitewash, the handprints of children pressed into wet cement next to a date celebrating new improvement on the sturdy old barn: 1949, 1956, 1962.

The old prophets would show us, beneath the dust and dirt, that here was once a kind of farming pleasing in the eyes of God. Here heaven and earth, storms and drought, grace and gratitude joined together to form a compelling matrix of thought, work and prayer. This intricate pattern of life yielded communities of abundant life, a life of planning, planting and prospering that enriched our nation with physical, moral and spiritual strength.

"May our barns overflow with every possible crop, may the sheep be counted in the thousands, may our cattle be strong and stout. Happy the nation of whom this is true. Happy the nation whose God is the Lord!" (Psalm 144)

Like the pin that joins mortise and tenon, the sacred word joins food and faith, abundant pastures and joyful cities, bread-giving wheat and life-giving Bread. And so the sturdy frames of old barns and the stubborn words of old prophets join together to form a structure of their own, a structure of thought in which we can explore some hard and difficult questions of today.

Amos and Hosea, Micah and Obadiah — they all know the questions we face, and they have the answers we seek.

For example, we ask "When does a legitimate profit overstep God's demand for justice?"

"Whenever God is not honored," they respond, "and children go hungry and rent on the trailer can't be paid."

But we grow uncomfortable with the implications and change the subject: "How can it be, as you prophets always claim, that good business destroys the fertility of the fields?"

"The answer is simple," they respond. "It happens whenever the gifts of creation are taken for granted. Look to the edges of your cities, where every hour of every day acres of farmland are scraped away."

"But there are times," we protest, "when efficiency must be increased."

And the prophets nod their heads in agreement.

"We know of what you speak," they say. "We've seen it happen many times. We know well what happens to civilizations when farming communities become expendable. Yes, indeed," they reply, "at such times in history, efficiency does a very thorough job of wiping out the farmers."

But with puzzled looks, the holy ones ask a question of their own: "What is so efficient," they wonder, "when food must travel 1,800 miles to find rest on your plate?"

And one last question they beg to raise, one question they seem most anxious to ask: "When will it happen," the prophets query, "if it ever will happen, that thanksgiving begins to transform your transacting?"

So plead the prophets of yesterday. Their words rustle the pages of trade agreements, corporate reports and lists of political contributors; their wisdom whistles like a cold wind across the prairie, blowing through the empty windows of large and once-beautiful houses.

But nostalgia is popular and close at hand. If you happen to find yourself paging through books of it, let the words of the prophets fill in what is missing beneath those glossy pictures of quaint old barns. There will be no animals nor farmers; there will be no hay nor grain. Swept clean away are any pictures of manure, missing limbs or maimed hands. Pictures that might make us think.

A Homily for Ed

The first time I went to visit Ed in the nursing home was in the fall of the year. He was looking out the large window next to his bed. Through this window he was able to see the neat houses and yards of one of the newer subdivisions on the west side of Coldwater. After we talked for a little while, he looked out the window again, and he told me that he had built many of those houses.

Ed was very proud of his work.

Ed was very much like those craftsmen we read about in the Book of Sirach, in a passage of Scripture that talks about craftsmen and people who work with their hands: the farmer, the blacksmith, the potter — and surely the carpenter and the contractor. "All these," it says, "put their trust in their hands and each is skilled at his own craft. A town could not be built without them. . . ."

Sirach goes on to say that these people do not have the prominence of lawyers or judges, but nonetheless it's their work that gives solidarity to the created world, and that for them, the work of their hands is their prayer to God.

It is extremely difficult for someone used to working with his hands, someone used to raising roof beams and putting up walls, to lay all that aside. We all knew it was difficult for Ed. This was but one of the many, many disappointments he faced as his strength and abilities became more and more limited.

As I rang the bell on Thursday morning, tolling it 48 times, one for each year of Ed's life, I was aware, toward the end, of the muscles in my arms getting tired and the bell beginning to toll more slowly. And at that time I found myself thinking of the last nine years of Ed's life, and how those years were long and difficult for him and his family. How much better it would be if we could all come to the end of our lives like the Prophet Elijah. When Elijah's work on this earth was finished, a fiery chariot came down from heaven and carried him off to the throne of God. It was simple and easy.

But it is not that way for most of us. And it certainly was not that way for Ed. For him, life would be more like a ride in a stagecoach than a fiery chariot: A bumpy ride, with many unscheduled stops. We all know that Ed liked working with his hands, but what some of us do not know was that he once made a replica of a stagecoach that now sits near the fireplace in his home. Like all of Ed's work, it's very well done, full of detail and put together just right. It was a task, I am sure, that took a good deal of time. And I think it can serve as a reminder to us that it is only with much determination and a lot of time and effort that people somehow manage to fit the pieces of their lives together. Unfortunately, sometimes the pieces just don't want to fit.

Ed was a craftsman and a carpenter. He knew how pieces are meant to fit together. But the last years of his life found him with many pieces that just wouldn't fit. And his trip to heaven was not at the side of Elijah on a fiery chariot. Rather, it was at the side of Christ — Christ on the cross. For you see, the pieces did not fit for Jesus either. When you and I gaze upon the cross, do we not see, in the broken body of Jesus, all the broken pieces of the world? We see a man who himself was broken. But we also see something else. We see a Savior who takes the world's sadness upon his shoulders. We see a Savior who knows the agony and pain that this life can contain. We see a Savior who will love us all the way through the pain and doubt of suffering and death.

It is into his knowing and loving arms that we commend our brother Ed. For in those arms is the promise that someday all our questions will be answered, all our pain will be healed, and all the pieces will be put right.

Winter

Advent:
A Season of Grace,
A Season of Thieves

The young boy stands before me confessing his sins. He avoids my eyes and focuses instead on the statue of Saint Nicholas peering over my shoulder. The boy's name is also Nicholas, and in a few days he will awaken to find a bowl on the kitchen table or one of his father's work socks hung on a door frame filled with candy, nuts and fruit.

This is the way Saint Nicholas visits the children in the town of Osgood on the eve of his feast, December 6. He is not only the patron of children, but also the patron of the local parish. Here the saintly bishop is honored for his kindness to children and also for assisting grownups in paying their bills. In the *Plotdeutch* of my elderly parishioners: *"Nicholaus brinks gilt en haus!"* (Nicholas brings money to the house.)

The Advent gospel readings may speak of a thief breaking into a home, but our patronal feast remembers a bishop breaking open a shutter to throw in bags of gold to three young girls. It's an oddly appropriate beginning to Advent, a season of grace and a season of thieves.

I place my hand on young Nicholas' head and my other hand on his shoulder. I speak the solemn words of absolution: "Through the ministry of the church, may God give you pardon and peace. . . ."

Tonight's liturgy is the first of many Advent penance services in my rural parishes. As always, I am deeply moved as my parishioners come forward to confess their sins. I am especially moved by the sincerity of the children. Their crimes, of course, are seldom more than petty thievery or sibling rivalry, but their faith in the grace of the sacrament is overwhelming.

As I speak the words of forgiveness, I feel the muscles in Nicholas' shoulders relax. He lowers his head as I bless him. At this angle of sight, I happen to notice how much he resembles his father: the firm line of his jaw, the serious shadows around his young eyes. I find myself imagining him years from now coming to confession on a December night with children of his own. The same stained-glass windows will loom above them, cold and gray with a winter wind whistling through their cracks. Same, too, will be the creaking of the pews in the quiet church, the examination of the soul, the resolve to avoid the near occasions of sin, the whispered words of release and relief.

All this discipline and mercy in a season of Advent wreaths and Jesse trees and socks of candy! All this devotion beneath the outstretched arms of Christ on the cross, the hands of a priest and the watchful gaze of a grandfatherly bishop!

With all the contemporary emphasis on such things as adult education, renewal programs and lay ministry training, I find the coming of December refreshing. I delight in the sudden surge of life in the domestic church as parish programs are shelved and other, more established "programs" take their place — caroling, decorating, preparing fruit baskets for the homebound, visiting grand-parents, going to confession, buying gifts for brothers, sisters and parents.

The commercial despoiling of the Advent season is ever present and ever regrettable, but there simply are no seminars or programs that can rival the spiritual potential of the month of December in the life of a family — or in that of a pastor.

In a country parish the change of seasons is directly related to the church's call for a change of heart. Conversion is, literally, in the air you breathe. There is the change of temperature, the change in daily chores, the early nightfall, the feel of new gloves on your hands, the feel of new things in the soul.

Here in the Midwest, the December air also brings a welcome silence. The snorting tractors and the raucous choppers are put away. The drying fans at the elevator no longer drone through the night. The first snowfall brings an almost palpable sense of stillness that only the most jaded soul fails to notice.

It is the silence, more than anything else, that readies the soul for the grace of Advent. I hear it in the strangest of places. I hear it between the sound of logs falling into the wood box next to my stove, and in the blackness that stretches between the stars in the winter sky. It settles amid the rustling sound of straw as I bed the stable for my sheep. A crimson sunset beyond a woods of gaunt, black trees calls silently to my eyes. The muffled stamping of my horse's hooves in the snow soothes me as I saddle up to ride into town for morning Mass.

So begins the month of December, a season with uniquely aural dimensions. Each season contains its own sensory catalysts for conversion, I think. In the spring it is the smell of newly turned earth, the scent of rain in the air and the fragrance of churches perfumed with Easter lilies. The summer moves in with the taste of salty sweat on one's lips and matures in the flavor of berries and sweet corn and warm tomatoes from the garden. Summer also favors the sense of touch with humidity pressing down on one's shoulders and warm breezes blowing through an opened shirt. The fall dazzles the eyes with the color of the leaves and the crisp clarity of the air. But the winter is made for the ear: Prophets cry out, carols are sung, phone calls are made to distant relatives and, with little effort, the soul discovers new levels of peace in the silence of the air and the softness of snow.

But as colorful lights begin to appear on the houses and families begin to bubble with activity, I notice a counter-movement within myself. It is then that I know that a deep conversion is in the offing. I begin to shore up my inner strength, for I know that my pastoral routine is about to change from programs to problems. The peaceful medi-tations of Advent will soon give way to prayers for troubled souls at Christmas.

I offer no estimate of the flow or timing of traumatic events in the world, and I would be loath to suggest that there is a greater occurrence of such things in the month of December. I only know that the feelings of despair, like those of joy, are intensified at this time of year.

I begin to experience this juxtaposition of joy and sorrow when odd associations enter my mind unexpectedly. I will find myself, for instance, puzzled by the current attraction of laissez-faire economics as I stare at a ceramic Victorian village in a store window. My mind will wander from the quaint depictions of stables and shepherds on the Christmas cards arranged on my desk to images of peas-ants in Chiapas or refugees in Rwanda or protesters at abortion clinics here in Ohio. My prayers at vespers will be interrupted by memories of my sins and the regrets of middle age. I will fixate on friends lost to misunderstandings, words spoken in anger, exploits of pride. These all come and sit by the fire with me as I wait for the inevitable calls that come fast and steady at this season: frantic calls from emergency rooms, anxious calls from troubled marriages, a drunken call from a friend at a bar trying to find his way out of the cold comfort of self-hatred.

As Advent gives way to Christmas, my spirit moves from the soothing silence of snowy fields to that of a darkening woods. The silence turns cold and bitter, punctuated by the groan and rub of branches in the wind. And it is here, on the dark side of December, that I realize I have, once again, come to Bethlehem by the way of the brigand.

Shepherds hear angelic songs, but I hear the moan of sin. Joseph hears voices in his dreams, but I do not dream. My spirit lopes through the woods, nervous and ravenous for the wounds of Christ to heal me and those who come to me. Like a thief trespassing in a hunter's cabin, I grab for objects in moonlight, sack drawers for drugs to heal the gnawing pain.

Thus I come, stumbling and desperate, to the Cave hoping to hear an echo of softness amid the stone. I come propelled by the force of sin and the fear of death etched in the faces of all the people of the world.

But here, at last, in the drafty grotto, I will come to discover God's gift of grace to desperate thieves. I will be the "good thief," this time stealing a place at the start of the gospel. Needing the knowledge that the blessed mystery is indeed commencing, the knowledge of the

Incarnation penetrating the world like shafts of ice into the black water of a backwoods pond. A cutting knowledge purifying all that is human and painful and weak.

It is then that I realize that this is what transpires in a season of grace. This is what relaxes the muscles in a proud man's neck. This is what inspires a young girl's careful positioning of figurines in a crèche. This remote reflection of heaven. This possibility of possessing God's possessions.

Scenes from a Search

It is the hour before dawn and we are sitting in my kitchen in silence. A dim bulb shines above the sink, turning the faded room into a yellow cavern where we huddle, like shell-shocked refugees, in the chill of a February morning.

A young man named Scott and his fiancée, Pam, have roused me from sleep and are waiting for me to accompany them to the firehouse where, we assume, a search effort is being organized.

Pam's face is pale and her posture is limp with fatigue. Scott is nervous and edgy. He glances toward the windows, his hands jammed into the pockets of his coat.

"I'm the one who gave her the idea," he says in a tight voice, shaking his head.

"What idea?" I ask.

"To take up running. Jogging for exercise."

"It's not your fault," mutters Pam. "It's no one's fault. It's . . . it's just unbelievable." Her voice trails off.

I notice tears welling up in Scott's eyes.

"We'll find her," I tell him. "We'll find your sister, Scott."

I go upstairs to wash my face and finish getting dressed. I grab a hat and coat, and the three of us leave by the back door. We pass behind the township house and walk across the gravel parking lot of the tavern behind my house.

A group of men in hunting fatigues meets us on the sidewalk. The sheriff's deputies are posting signs on the storefronts. Along the street there are livestock trailers with horses stamping to get out. There are pickups with all-terrain vehicles strapped to their beds.

Amid the activity, I happen to notice on a strip of grass near the corner of the firehouse the body of a kitten nestled in a peaceful pose. A fine sparkling of frost on its fur tells me that it has died in its sleep.

The white light of dawn stabs at the buildings and our village is awakening to a day of frightening portent.

Police Search for Missing Teen

NORTH STAR — Darke County deputies are in search of clues today into the possible abduction of a 19-year-old girl.

According to Sgt. Det. John Heiser of the Darke County Sheriff's Office, missing is Terry Lane of North Star, Ohio.

Lane is described as a white female, 5'4" tall, 154 pounds, brown hair and brown eyes. She was last seen jogging in the area of Cohee Road, south of the village Saturday around 8:10 A.M. Her

64

Walkman, which she carried along with her when she jogs, was found by relatives on Rismiller Road east of her home.
Greenville Daily Advocate
February 23, 1998

It is close to midnight but the small house is filled with relatives and neighbors. Outside, sheriff's cruisers are patrolling the roads, stopping now and then to shine lights beneath bridges and into culverts. A helicopter hovers over a nearby woods, its pounding thud sounding like distant thunder. Its spotlight floats like a phantom amid the branches of the barren trees.

Terry's parents are hopeful. There is an air of tense expectation. Everyone has questions. Everyone tries to be encouraging. But conversations are muted and silence predominates. Everyone, it seems, is troubled by terrible thoughts they try hard to repress.

We begin to pray the Sorrowful Mysteries of the Rosary. People kneel where there is room. We pray quietly and slowly. A deputy comes to the door and stands with head bowed as we remember Jesus' agony. We pray that his cup of suffering will not spill on the door of this house. We pray carefully and deliberately, as though the familiar cadence of our words will bring some sense of order into this tense and tedious night. We pray that Jesus' scourging and torture will suffice and supplant those fears we try not to imagine in our minds.

Search for Teen Continues

NORTH STAR — "Shocked." That's the word that can describe the reaction of community members here after hearing word that a 19-year-old woman may have been abducted from a rural country road southeast of this village.

Neighbors, relatives and friends of Terry Lane have been doing all they can to help the Lane family find their loved one.

Over the weekend, neighbors helped investigators search for the girl's whereabouts without any luck. By late Saturday evening flyers were distributed in nearby towns in search of leads.

"You can't believe something like this would happen in your own backyard," said Kim Singer, manager of the North Star 1-Stop. "The whole community has come together to help with the search."

Jim Brinkman was one of the residents who searched for the teenager Saturday night and Sunday morning. His family is close friends with the Lane family.

"It's unbelievable that something like this would happen in an area like ours," he said.

Greenville Daily Advocate
February 24, 1998

The search is well organized. Maps of contiguous counties are prepared, section by section, township by township. People walk slowly across the fields. Those with horses search the woods and river banks. We are told to look for a patch of blue clothing or a Walkman headset. We are told to report anything suspicious.

We search farm buildings, gullies, well pits, abandoned cars and hunters' shacks back in the hills. We are told not to search alone.

Factories dismiss their workers to allow them to join the search.

Each morning, coffee is made and food is set out on tables. Shifts of volunteers are assigned to staff the headquarters.

Each morning, prayers are offered, and the searchers set out. The number of volunteers is overwhelming.

Initially, the sheriff thinks it might be a lark. He speculates that Terry might be holing up with an old boyfriend. But he does not know Terry. He does not know her parents or her family. He has not worshiped with Terry at Mass Sunday after Sunday. He had not conversed with her about God and life and the sacredness of human love.

We all wish that he was correct in his assessment. But we all know that he is wrong, very wrong.

We watch our town on the local news. We see it shown from the air, our neat houses surrounding our quaint little church. The scene switches to one of the local bars. We are surprised at how grizzled some of us look. We laugh at the way we struggle to answer the obvious and stupid questions posed by the reporters.

Search Extends Nationwide.
$10,000 Reward Offered for Information
NORTH STAR — Darke County Sheriff Joe
Veldman said as word of Terry Lane's disappearance
spread nationally, hundreds upon hundreds of phone
calls have flooded the sheriff's department lines.

   "We're getting a lot of calls from out-of-state,
but none of them have been actual sighting reports
of her," he said.

   Most of the calls, according to Veldman, are
reports of suspicious vehicles/activities.
   Greenville Daily Advocate
   February 25, 1998

The glow of vesper light fills the church and a cloud
of incense rises about the Easter candle. We sing of Israel's
sojourn and pray for the light of Christ to be a lamp unto
our feet.

Nothing looks familiar in the dark. Everything seems
strange. Darkness has come to this community. We look
around us and see that this place is no longer our home.

The rich soil and pleasant towns of western Ohio have
become a foreign place. I hear about guns being loaded
and kept on the night stands. Children are afraid to fall
asleep. No one walks alone. Everyone is overwhelmed.

Can this be the community we once knew?

Tonight's words from the apostle Paul hit us hard:
"We are strangers in an alien land."

What does he mean?

He means that there are times and circumstances
when God's people will feel completely lost. Times when

we have no vocabulary to express the thoughts we harbor. Times when we have no sense of direction and no one can be trusted. And all we want to do is go home!

The bread we eat is thin and flat. Our legs are weak from walking. Our eyes are tired from looking. Our skin is torn by thorns and brush.

But we do not travel alone. We sojourn as God's people. Like Israel in the desert, we follow an obscure and distant cloud.

And hidden in that cloud is the Savior. His presence briefly detected like sparks of flame within the smoke. His sacred promises keeping the fearful night from utterly engulfing us.

He is the Bread that we gather from amid the hot rock and dead brush of this desert place.

He is our Moses calling us onward to a better country than the one we now know.

He is our God, our only hope. Taking us home where we belong. Leading us home where we long to be.

Family Speaks about Missing Teen

NORTH STAR — Bernice Lane is confident that her daughter is still alive. "We just have to find her," said the mother of the rural North Star teen who has been missing since Saturday morning. "We won't give up until we find her."

Bernice said she was seated on the love seat in their living room when her 19-year-old daughter, Terry, set out to go jogging in the vicinity of their home.

"I saw her go out the door," remarked Bernice, who doesn't remember anything else that occurred

that day out of the ordinary other than the
subsequent disappearance of her daughter.

Terry is a feeding assistant at the Brethren's
Home. She did not show up for work on Saturday.
"After she left the house, I went to morning Mass.
When I came home, I presumed that she had gone
on to work," said her mother.

Greenville Daily Advocate
February 27, 1998

The family pleads for Terry's release. No one knows
who could possibly have done this. Psychics offer their
services. Rumors begin to circulate.

A car passes a group of searchers in a field and a
man leans out of its window yelling obscene things, using
Terry's name. His voice screeches like a bat in the air,
his ugly language spreading demon filth across our fields.

Houses are locked for the first time in years. There
are reports of suspicious characters, rumors of possible
suspects. The grade school is on alert for hostage-taking.
Farmers are nervous about going into their barns in
the dark of morning. Parents are frantic. No one can keep
their minds on anything but this.

Is Terry still alive? Is she being fed? How far away might
she be? How close is the perpetrator?

Was he some stranger driving along the highway? Has
he returned to search with us?

Would appearances betray an abductor? Or have we
sung hymns together in church?

Investigation Continues into Second Week
NORTH STAR — Since last Saturday thousands
have turned out to volunteer their time to search
wooded areas, abandoned structures, waterways
and fields across Darke, Auglaize, Mercer and
Randolph, Indiana counties.

For those places not accessible by foot,
helicopters, horses and four-wheel vehicles have
been used.

The search for the girl continued into the
weekend as plans were made for a prayer service
tonight at the St. Louis Catholic Church in this
village.

Early on in the investigation, Sheriff Joe
Veldman called in the Federal Bureau of Investi-
gation and the Bureau of Criminal Identification
and Investigation to assist in the case.
Greenville Daily Advocate
March 1, 1998

Some friends and I head to the St. Mary's River with
our horses. We are thirty miles from North Star. We know
that a girl from the nearby town was abducted about a
year ago and that her remains were recently found not far
from where we are.

The man at the gravel pit where we unload our
horses from the trailer reminds us of this unsettling fact.
He takes us inside his office and shows us the location
where the girl was found on a map hanging on the wall.
The map is faded to a sepia color and so is the room.
There is the scraping of grit on the floor beneath our
boots as we shuffle toward the wall. Our dusters smell
of horses and woodsmoke, and I suddenly remember

a historical marker along a canal not far from here. It tells about "Bloody Bridge," where one man decapitated another in a fight over a woman in the 1800s.

I try to resist thinking of Terry being dead but today I am beginning to lose hope. The wider the search becomes the more hopeless our efforts seem. But no one mentions giving up. "We'll keep searching until she's found," every-one assures the family. But I am beginning to wonder how long the effort will last.

We mount up and ride toward the slow and shallow river. Another day of looking for something we don't want to find. The days of searching have left me drained; I cannot imagine how the family is holding up. Terry's mother refuses to leave the house for fear of missing a phone call from the abductor. Her father and brothers spend every waking hour plodding through fields and woods with groups of volunteers.

Last night I drove to my barn to feed my sheep and horses. There had been a community meeting at the church and the hour was late. When I switched on the light, I was startled at the sight of a young colt that had acciden-tally hanged herself. Her golden neck was wedged between apost and the hinge of a gate; her glassy eyes bore the traces of unmistakable horror. I was stunned. She had been so beautiful, so tame.

As I collected the buckets and poured in the grain
I began to cry. I ended up sobbing for hours. Uncontrollable.
I wasn't crying over my horse but for myself and my
community and over everything that was happening to us.

Today I am bone-tired. But the sun is shining and I am
grateful for the quiet company of the friends who are
with me. Two of them are factory workers, and one owns
a tavern. We are proud of our horses and proud of the
outpouring of support and compassion within our community. But deep down, like the rivulets of this brown river,
run muddy strains of confusion and frustration.

I lead my gelding onto a sand bar where his hooves
begin to sink into the mud. He suddenly panics and begins
lunging frantically for solid ground. He climbs the bank,
then dives into a stand of trees and brush. I manage to stay
in the saddle but several vines are strung across my chest
before I am able to calm my horse. For a moment we
can't move, and I feel the strictures about my body.

I look around for my friends but they are gone. The
flood plain is dank and sour and full of litter, and I find
myself wondering where Terry is being held, what fear is
racing through her mind, what sort of strictures are
wrapped about her body.

I am coaxing the horse out of the thicket when I hear
Brent and Randy calling for me and Gene.

We meet up in a section of a cornfield that pushes
like a narrow finger between a woods and the river, out

of sight of any road. Tire tracks are visible along the river bank. They lead up to a square of freshly-turned earth.

There are obvious signs that a remaining mound of dirt has been shoveled away, presumably loaded into the vehicle. The tracks then head across the field toward a country road.

We study the scene from all angles and discuss it at length. This can't be a grave, but what else would it be? We can't come up with any other explanation. Randy and Brent guard the site while Gene and I ride back to the gravel pit to call the sheriff.

When the deputies come to excavate the scene, they find only the partial leg of a deer.

We are relieved but incredulous. My friends are hunters and this makes no sense to them. Why such a large grave for a part of a leg? Why would someone go to the trouble of hiding something so inconsequential? If the deer had been poached, it was not stripped clean. And if it was poached, where was the rest of it?

I stop at Gene's bar later that evening. Randy and Brent are there. They are drinking down beer and spitting out anger.

"I'll find her," says Brent. "If it takes a year, I'll find her."

"And the bastard who took her," says Randy, "is going to pay."

Search Ends Tragically

NEW WESTON — Darke County Sheriff Joe Veldman described the tragic end of the 14-day search for Terry Lane as his worst nightmare.

"I don't know what to say. It's a tragic, tragic event for our county," said Veldman.

Investigators found what they believe to be the remains of Lane buried in a field along McFeely-Petry Road near New Weston around 1:15 p.m. Friday afternoon. Authorities found her dead, buried nearly six feet underground near a gravel pit.

Their only suspect is James Whitman, 43, of the same address. Whitman, supposedly convicted of rape twice in the past, was reported to have no connection to Terry Lane.

Search volunteers previously had walked through the field where she was found, but failed to notice anything unusual.

"The site was not obvious," said Veldman. "The perpetrator went to great lengths to avoid detection."

Greenville Daily Advocate
March 7, 1998

Karl, Terry's father, has asked me to go to the place where they found her and pray the prayers of commendation. It is late Friday afternoon, and I speak the words across a grid-like expanse of trenches. I stand alone against a yellow plastic ribbon strung by the deputies, praying the ancient prayers of the church.

Go forth, faithful Christian. I commend you, my dear sister, to almighty God and entrust you to your Creator. May you return to him who formed you from the dust of the earth. Go forth, faithful Christian.

The ground here is hard clay and Terry's body was buried beneath a pile of brush and fallen trees. Nearby there is a stagnant pond with a barren tree leaning over the gray water.

A large area of ground had been previously disturbed, as though a small woods had been cleared for a field. This sort of excavation is common. Searchers would notice nothing unusual.

I return to the ritual book. My voice sounds as thin as smoke in the cold air and I wonder if such a place can be made whole again, the evil done to this soil transformed by the presence of an innocent victim, the air cleansed by the scattering of sacred syllables upon the wind.

May holy Mary, the angels and all the saints
come to meet you . . .

The deputies and detectives have stopped their digging and are waiting for forensic experts to arrive before removing Terry's body from the earth.

I am not sure where her body is. I direct my words out across the disturbed landscape.

Go forth, faithful Christian.
May you live in peace this day,
may your home be with God in Zion,
with Mary, the virgin Mother of God,
with Joseph, and all the angels and saints.

Is it possible for the family of saints to rejoice in heaven when a family here is in such pain?

I see a mother cradling her infant in her arms. I see a little girl running to the arms of her father. I see Terry at the county fair laughing with her friends. I see her quilts, her water colors, her pets, her sister's swing in the back yard, her brothers' tears of rage, her grandmother's weary face.

In this wretched place, so rough and brutal in the winter light, the Evil One seems to sneer in victory: God's earth clawed and scarred; a living temple of his Spirit destroyed and discarded like rubbish into a pit of cold, wet clay. The prayers grow more difficult.

I commend you, my dear sister, to almighty God. May Christ who was crucified for you bring you freedom and peace. May Christ who died for you admit you into his garden of paradise. May Christ the good Shepherd acknowledge you as one of his flock.

All we can do is cry and pray. All we can do in this land of exile, in this valley of tears is cry, cry for deliverance. And soon the rite takes up that desperate chant:

Deliver your servant, Lord, from every distress!
As you delivered Noah from the flood . . .
as you delivered Abraham from Ur of the Chaldees . . .
as you delivered Job from his sufferings . . .
Moses from the hand of Pharoah . . .
Daniel from the den of lions . . .
the three young men from the fiery furnace . . .
Susanna from her false accusers . . .
as you delivered David from the attacks of Saul and Goliath . . .
as you delivered Peter and Paul from prison.
Deliver your servant, Lord, through Jesus our Savior
who suffered death for us and gave us eternal life!

I hear a helicopter approaching, and reporters are beginning to gather along the road in the distance.

I close the book and slowly kneel down.

I touch my face. I touch the ground. I beg. I beg for the touch of God.

A Blessing for Clair

"Her name is Clair."

It was my nephew's voice on the phone.

"You should see her, Jim. She's beautiful. Real beautiful."

And so is her name, I thought to myself.

"Wait until your grandfather finds out about this," I said, imagining my father receiving the news of a great-granddaughter named Clair, the name of the woman who shared his life for fifty-six years.

"Are you at home?" I ask. "Is everything okay? How is Brenda?"

"Everybody's fine," he said. "I'm headed back to the hospital now. We'll call you about baptism."

I could see Doug at the phone in the kitchen of their old farm house, wearing his coveralls and smelling of cows.

He would still be in his outdoor clothes because their kitchen is cold and drafty this time of year. He and Brenda invested in building a dairy barn when they were married. For now, any extra money goes into the farm, not the house.

Nevertheless, Clair will have a home warm with the love of her parents, a brother named Ted and a sister named Katerri. As she grows, she will have days full of work, just like her parents, her grandparents and great-grandparents.

Unfortunately, the trends of agribusiness do not favor the long-term prosperity of the family farm. The qualities so important for rural communities — faith, compassion and resilience — matter little to the planners of industrialized food production.

Children like Clair and her brother and sister are in the balance. The biblical wisdom that says that the way we treat the land determines how we treat one another is again proving itself true in our culture of ultra-efficiency and social decline.

But I am confident that Clair will know that she is far more than a mere producer and consumer of goods. After all, the water of holy baptism will soon flow over her, and the love of the Trinity will enfold her.

She will have the rare honor of tramping after her father and mother in fields where flinty arrowheads can still be found glinting in the sun after a spring rain.

She will grow up knowing, as well, that war was waged upon this land. There are fields nearby where cannonballs and pieces of artillery can be found alongside the arrowheads and tomahawks of the Shawnee.

But beneath this scarred and productive land is life-giving water, a water table, pure and silent, from which Clair and all succeeding generations must draw. It is this water drawn from deep in the earth that gives me hope.

Recently I discovered a well while walking along the remnants of the Miami and Erie Canal on a Sunday afternoon. The place is near my brother's farm, my home place, not far from the town of Fort Loramie. This well is over a century old. It was made of chinked fieldstone and its walls are still as straight as a plumb line.

My grandmother often talked about a hotel that once stood along the canal serving immigrants who were coming north from the Ohio River at Cincinnati. Chancing upon the well of that old hotel took me by surprise. I have long been intrigued by the history of the canal, which ran between Toledo and Cincinnati and was completed in 1849. But unlike the stagnant water upon which boats and possessions and settlers were carried, the water from this now-abandoned well would be fresh. It would slake the thirst of the immigrants and wash their skin and refresh their mules.

Eventually, the water from such stone wells would also be found in the baptismal fonts of the immigrants' churches. For these people, like all people before them, would carry within them the eternal thirst for God. And in their rites of water and rebirth the undying dream of God's reign would be instilled, a small but tempering influence against the gods of greed and gore, exploitation and extermination.

Years later, in a field about a hundred yards from this well, bands of Gypsies would camp in the bottom ground. This would be in the time of my grandfather. His daughters, Clara and Loretta, would be hidden in a closet for fear the Gypsies would steal them. Yet despite the prejudice, hay and grain were given to the people in the colorful clothes to feed their livestock.

This is one of the many stories we must remember to pass on to young Clair. The memory of grace amid sin and fear, the knowledge of salvation, like a transparent stream flowing unseen among the veins of limestone and shale beneath the fields of arrowheads and horseshoes, corn and wheat.

For the God of water and sky, seasons and growth, food and faith, is, dear Clair, more ancient than the land and stronger than the sun. Honor the Lord, Clair, honor the Lord your God as you will come to honor your father, your mother, your life, your soul.

Then your world will be blessed. And the land shall be blessed. And, in God's good time, all people shall be blessed. Blessed with pure water and good faith. Blessed with a history. Blessed with peace. Blessed with justice.

Blessed through all seasons. Blessed through all time.